READING POWER

Helping Organizations

Doctors Without Borders

Anastasia Suen

The Rosen Publishing Group's
PowerKids Press™
New York

Published in 2002 by The Rosen Publishing Group, Inc.
29 East 21st Street, New York, NY 10010

First Edition

Book Design: Michelle Innes

Photo Credits: Cover, pp. 4, 6, 8–17 courtesy of MSF;
p. 19 courtesy of David Kaisel/MSF; pp. 20–21 courtesy of Mike Goldwater/MSF.

Suen, Anastasia.
Doctors without Borders / by Anastasia Suen.
   p. cm. — (Helping organizations)
Includes index.
ISBN 0-8239-6002-1 (library binding)
1. Medical assistance—Developing countries—Juvenile literature. 2.
Humanitarian assistance—Developing countries—Juvenile literature. 3.
International relief—Developing countries—Juvenile literature. 4.
Médecins sans frontières (Association)—Juvenile literature. [1.
Doctors without Borders (Association)] I. Title.
RA390.F8 S84 2001
610'.6'01—dc21

                                   2001000557

Manufactured in the United States of America

Contents

Doctors Without Borders 4

Volunteers 8

Helping Others 12

Earthquake 18

Glossary 22

Resources 23

Index 24

Word Count 24

Note 24

Doctors Without Borders

In 1971, a group of doctors in France wanted to work together to help people all over the world. They started Doctors Without Borders.

These are some of the people who started Doctors Without Borders.

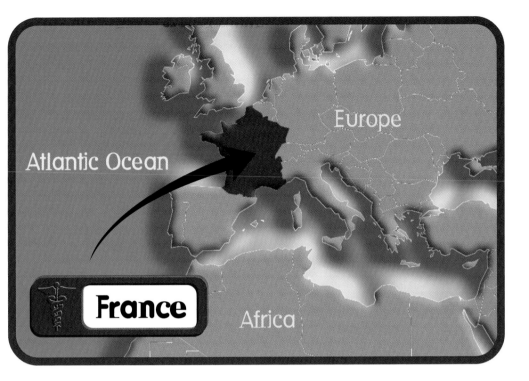

Europe

Atlantic Ocean

France

Africa

It's a Fact

Doctors Without Borders is *Médecins Sans Frontières* in the French language.

Today, Doctors Without Borders works in more than 80 countries. It helps people in wars and disasters.

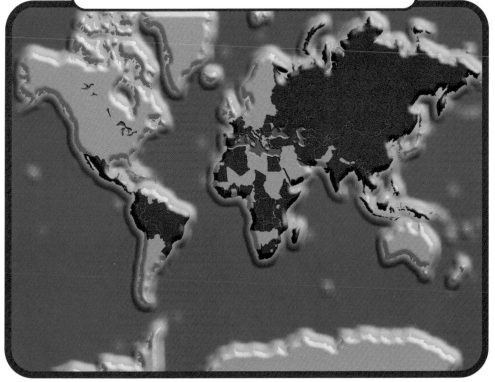

Doctors Without Borders at Work

Volunteers

Both men and women volunteer to work for Doctors Without Borders. These volunteers help many people.

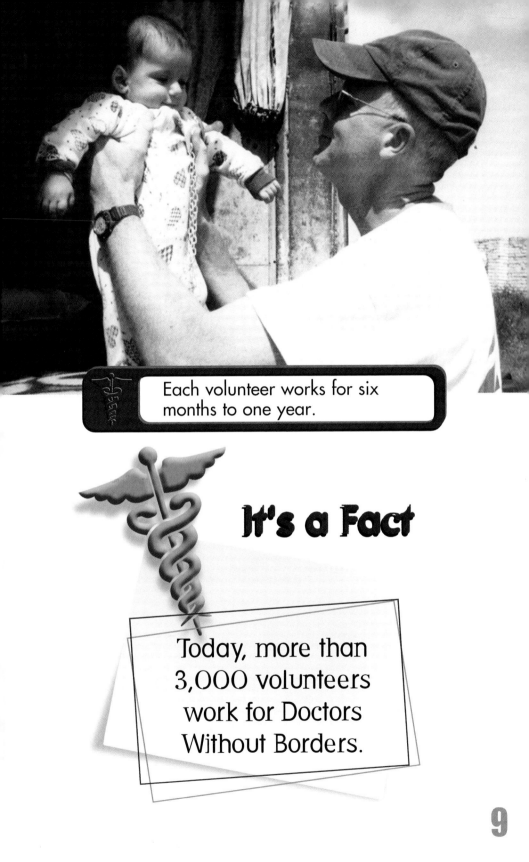

Each volunteer works for six months to one year.

It's a Fact

Today, more than 3,000 volunteers work for Doctors Without Borders.

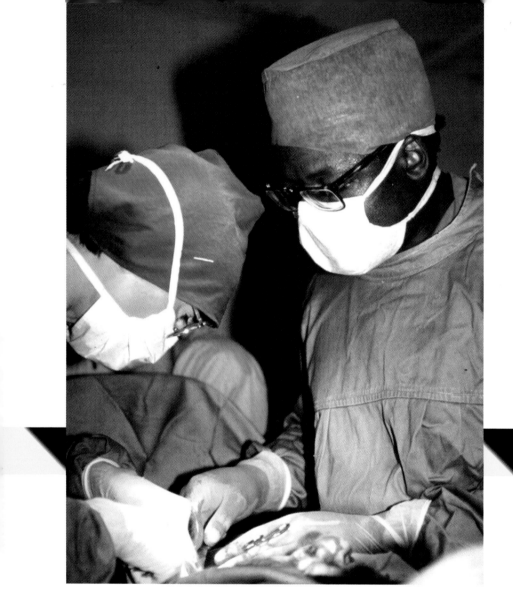

Some volunteers are doctors. Some are nurses. They help people who are sick or hurt.

Not all volunteers are doctors or nurses. Some help by moving supplies from place to place.

Helping Others

When a war starts, Doctors Without Borders comes to help. It helps people on both sides of the war.

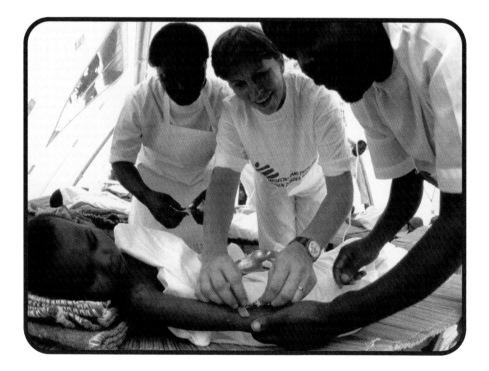

Volunteers bring supplies to people who need help.

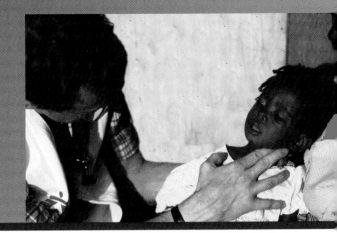

Doctors Without Borders goes where people need doctors. Some places do not have any doctors! Doctors Without Borders gives people the help that they need.

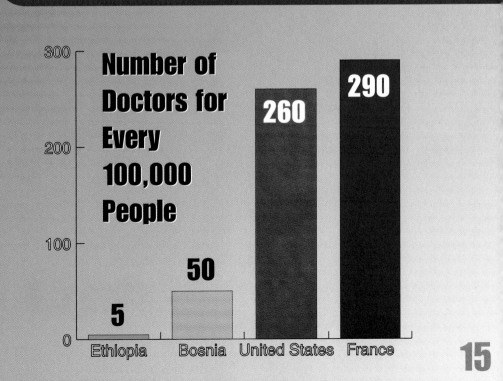

Number of Doctors for Every 100,000 People

Ethiopia	Bosnia	United States	France
5	50	260	290

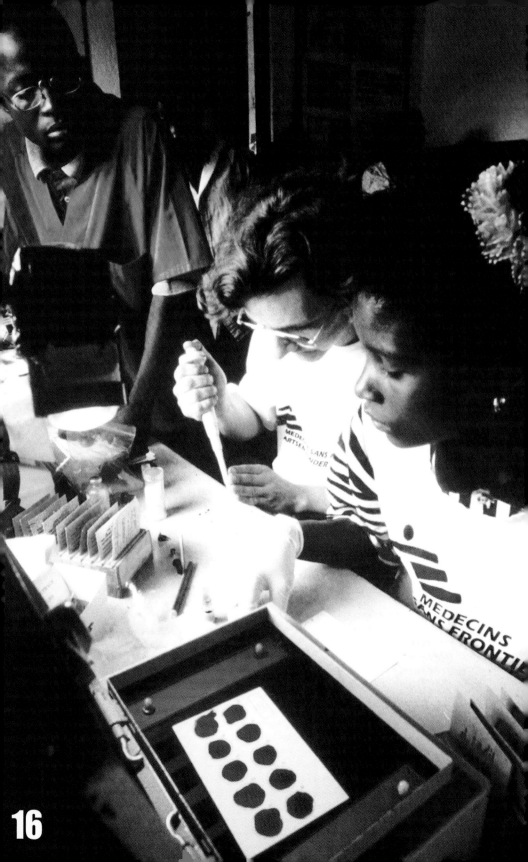

Doctors Without Borders volunteers work together to get medicine ready. Then they bring the medicine to people who are sick.

Atlantic Ocean

Pacific Ocean

South America

Colombia

Earthquake

In 1999, Doctors Without Borders helped people after an earthquake in Colombia. Volunteers brought medicine and medical supplies to the people there.

Doctors Without Borders volunteers helped about 80,000 people in Colombia. Doctors Without Borders helps millions of people every year.

Glossary

disasters (duh-**zas**-tuhrz) sudden events that cause great loss

earthquake (**erth**-kwayk) a shaking and shifting of the ground

Médecins Sans Frontières (mehd-**san son** frohn-tee-**air**) "Doctors Without Borders" in the French language

medicine (**mehd**-uh-suhn) something used to treat or prevent sickness

supplies (suh-**plyz**) materials used or given out when needed

volunteers (vahl-uhn-**tihrz**) people who work without pay

Resources

Books

When I Grow Up I Want to Be a Doctor
by Charles H. Ripp
Dorrance Publishing Company, Inc. (1997)

A Day in the Life of a Doctor
by Mary Bowman-Kruhm and
Claudine G. Wirths
The Rosen Publishing Group (1997)

Web Site

Doctors Without Borders for Kids
http://www.doctorswithoutborders.org/
   outreach/bol/Html/kids.html

Index

C
Colombia, 18, 20

D
disasters, 6

E
earthquake, 18

F
France, 4–5

M
medicine, 17–18
Médecins Sans Frontières, 5

S
supplies, 11, 13, 18

V
volunteers, 8–11, 13, 17–18, 20

W
war, 6, 12

Word Count: 214

Note to Librarians, Teachers, and Parents

If reading is a challenge, Reading Power is a solution! Reading Power is perfect for readers who want high-interest subject matter at an accessible reading level. These fact-filled, photo-illustrated books are designed for readers who want straightforward vocabulary, engaging topics, and a manageable reading experience. With clear picture/text correspondence, leveled Reading Power books put the reader in charge. Now readers have the power to get the information they want and the skills they need in a user-friendly format.